ANDY MURRAY BIOGRAPHY

A Champion's Journey: Triumph, Perseverance, and the Unwavering Pursuit of Greatness.

Michal E. Erickson

All right reserved .No part of this publication may be reproduced, distributed or transmitted in any form or by any means, including photocopying, recording,or other electronic or mechanical methods, without the prior written permission of the publisher, expect in the case of brief quotation embodied uncritical reviews and certain other non-commercial uses permitted by copyright law.

Copyright ©. Michal E. Erickson, 2024.

TABLE OF CONTENTS

OVERVIEW

CHAPTER 1: EARLY LIFE.

EARLY LIFE AND FAMILY BACKGROUND

OVERVIEW OF TENNIS.

EARLY GUIDANCE AND GROWTH.

CHAPTER 2: JUNIOR TENNIS CAREER

ACHIEVEMENTS IN JUNIOR TEAMS.

ASCEND TO WORLD NO. 1 IN JUNIOR WORLD

EXCHANGE TO PROFESSIONAL TENNIS.

CHAPTER 3: EARLY PROFESSIONAL CAREER.

EARLY PROFESSIONAL GAME AND SUCCESS.

A COMPLETION IN THE ATP TOURNAMENTS.

FAILURES AND RESETTLEMENTS.

CHAPTER 4: GRAND SLAM SUCCESS.

FIRST AWARD FOR GRAND SLAM AT US OPEN.

FIRST AWARD FOR GRAND SLAM AT US OPEN.

BRITISH HISTORY AND THE VICTORY AT WIMBLEDON.

OPEN AUSTRALIA'S VICTORY.

CHAPTER 5: OLYMPIC GLORY.

2012 LONDON GOLD MEDALS.

DEFENSE OF THE RIO 2016 GOLD MEDALS.

OLYMPIC LEGACY AND SIGNIFICANCE.

CHAPTER 6: COACHING AND TEAM.

COLLABORATION WITH IVAN LENDL

OTHER MENTORS AND COACHES.

AID THE FAMILY AND THE TEAM.

CHAPTER 7: INJURIES AND CHALLENGES.

RECOVERY AND BACK SURGERY.

OTHER INJURIES AND SETBACKS.

MENTAL FITNESS AND SUCCESS.

CHAPTER 8: OFF-COURT VENTURES.

CHARITY WORK AND PHILANTHROPY.

PERSONAL LIFE AND INTERESTS.

CHAPTER 9: LAW AND IMPACT.

IMPACT ON TENNIS IN BRITAIN.

INSPIRATION AND ROLE MODEL.

CONTRIBUTIONS FROM THE TENNIS INDUSTRY.

CHAPTER 10: LATER CAREER AND RETIREMENT.

SUBSEQUENT TOURS ON THE ATP TOUR.

FUTURE PLANS AND RETIREMENT.

THOUGHTS ON A SUCCESSFUL PROFESSION.

CONCLUSIONS.

OVERVIEW

The biography of Andy Murray provides a thorough and captivating overview of his life and career and a special window into the world of professional tennis. The biography expertly combines details from Murray's early years, his ascent to prominence, and his time as a tennis champion to provide a vivid picture of his commitment, tenacity, and love for the game.

The biography's ability to fairly balance Murray's personal and professional lives and present a complex and multidimensional picture of the tennis star is one of its strongest points. Murray's relationships with his family, coaches, and teammates are deftly examined by the author, who also reveals the complex web of support and direction that has shaped Murray's career.

The biography also explores Murray's physical and mental challenges, including his fights with depression and injury. These open stories show the emotional and psychological costs associated with performing at the highest level and provide a unique window into the difficulties faced by professional athletes.

Murray's narrative comes to life throughout the biography thanks to the author's use of vivid descriptions and captivating anecdotes, which let the reader feel as though they are sharing in Murray's highs and lows. Both fans and non-fans will find the biography to be enjoyable to read because of the writing's clarity, conciseness, and accessibility.

The biography delves into Murray's influence on the tennis community as well, highlighting his impact on upcoming players and his contributions to the expansion and advancement of the game. The author emphasizes Murray's philanthropic and charity endeavors, highlighting his unwavering devotion to giving back to the community and changing the world for the better.

Anyone interested in tennis, sports, or inspirational tales should read the biography. It provides a rare look into the life of a tennis winner and highlights the passion, tenacity, and hard work needed to succeed. The book solidifies Murray's status as one of the all-time great tennis players and attests to his lasting legacy.

CHAPTER 1: EARLY LIFE.

On May 15, 1987, Andy Murray was born in Glasgow, Scotland, to Judy and William Murray. His mother was a tennis coach, and his father, a former football player and tennis aficionado, had a small business in the area. When Andy was just ten years old, his parents got divorced, and his father eventually got married again.

Growing up in Dunblane, a small hamlet, Murray forged close relationships with his brother Jamie, who would go on to play professional tennis. Judy coached the brothers at the neighborhood tennis club, and their mother had always encouraged them to play the game.

Andy went to Dunblane High School after finishing Dunblane Primary School. In addition to being a great student, he loved sports, especially football and tennis. His first tennis coach was his mother, Judy, who was instrumental in developing his skill.

Murray has had a natural ability to play tennis from an early age. At the age of five, he won his first competition, and he went on to win other junior titles in

Scotland. His early development as a tennis player was greatly influenced by his mother's coaching and direction.

Although Andy Murray was regarded as a quiet and reserved young man, his love of tennis gave him the confidence and strong work ethic he needed to succeed. His tenacity and resolve would come to define his professional life. He would frequently practice his serves and volleys with his brother or smack balls against a wall as he spent hours perfecting his shots. His future success in the tennis world was made possible by his devotion to the game and his enjoyment of it.

EARLY LIFE AND FAMILY BACKGROUND

 Andy Murray grew up with a strong sense of community and family. From an early age, he was imbued with a strong work ethic and a passion for sports by his parents, Judy and William. The Murrays were well-known for their athletic ability; Andy's grandpa, Roy Erskine, played football professionally.

Andy's early exploits were set against the magnificent backdrop of rolling hills and picturesque landscape that surrounded him as he was growing up in Dunblane. He played with his brother, Jamie, for hours on end, building a relationship that would last a lifetime.

Andy's passion for sports was fostered by his parents; Judy, his mother, took him to the local tennis club. Andy's early athletic development was also greatly influenced by his father, William, who was an avid football player. Andy's early years were shaped by his family's encouragement and love, which laid the groundwork for his future success.

The Murrays were deeply rooted in history and customs as well. Andy was first exposed to the world of music and art by his skilled musician mother, Shirley Erskine. Andy's horizons were expanded, and his artistic side was shaped by this exposure.

Even with all the conveniences of small-town living, Andy had difficulties growing up. When he was just ten years old, his parents divorced, which was a trying time for him, but the love and support of his family got him through it.

All things considered, Andy Murray's early years and family history had a big impact on his character, work ethic, and love of sports. His family's love and support enabled him to grow into a gifted and committed young athlete who was prepared to take on the world.

OVERVIEW OF TENNIS.

Andy Murray's life turned around in a fortunate way when he was introduced to tennis. When he found a tennis racket in his garage when he was three years old, his interest was sparked. After realizing he was interested, his mother, Judy, started hitting balls with him in their backyard.

Judy began taking Andy to the nearby Dunblane tennis club, where she had played tennis herself, as his interest in the game grew. Andy's innate potential was noticed by Leon Smith, the club's coach, who started mentoring him. Andy's technique improved under Smith's tutelage, and he quickly became addicted to the game.

The backyard of the Murray family was transformed into an unofficial tennis court, where Andy and his brother Jamie fought back and forth. Judy, their mother, would frequently participate and offer advice and support.

These unofficial sessions helped Andy develop his abilities and gave him a spirit of competition that would help him in his future endeavors.

With his love for the game growing, Andy started to watch professional tennis matches on television, becoming enthralled by players like Pete Sampras, Boris Becker, and Andre Agassi. He observed their methods, evaluating their advantages and disadvantages, and harbored the hope of eventually enlisting in them.

Andy's discovery of tennis was not merely a fortuitous meeting; it would ultimately determine his fate. His life revolved around the sport, which gave him the motivation and sense of purpose he needed to become a champion.

EARLY GUIDANCE AND GROWTH.

Andy Murray's tennis career was greatly influenced by his early instruction and growth. Andy's first coach, Leon Smith, helped him refine his techniques and build a solid foundation in the game. Andy was able to establish a strong foundation that would serve him well in the future because of Smith's attention to technique and footwork.

Judy, Andy's mother, became increasingly involved in his coaching as his skills and commitment were recognised. Judy, a talented player and coach in her own right, gave Andy individualised attention and direction that improved his game and helped him cultivate a winning mindset.

Andy Murray's tennis growth was consistently supported by the Murray family. William, his father, gave up his own time and energy to support his son's ambition by driving him to training sessions and competitions. Andy was able to thrive because of the supportive environment that the family as a whole established.

But Andy's early training wasn't without its difficulties. On the court, he frequently lost his temper and became frustrated when he made mistakes or faced defeats. But with the enduring help of his family and the understanding direction of his coaches, Andy discovered how to control his feelings and focus his energies on personal development.

As Andy approached his preteen years, his trainers started exposing him to increasingly sophisticated methods and approaches. He gained the ability to craft his own playing style, outwitting his rivals by combining skill and ferocity. Andy's efforts were rewarded when his ranking started to climb and he gained recognition in Scottish and British tennis circles.

CHAPTER 2: JUNIOR TENNIS CAREER

Andy Murray's incredible junior tennis career demonstrated his talent, commitment, and tenacity. Murray encountered many chances and obstacles that influenced his growth as he went from a bright young player to a top-tier junior contender.

Murray earned his first junior title in the Scottish Junior Championships in 1999, when he was just 12 years old. With this triumph, he launched an amazing run of junior competitions in which he continuously showed off his talent and willpower.

Murray was chosen for the Great Britain junior national squad as a result of his achievements in junior tennis. He had the opportunity to compete at the highest level and obtain priceless experience by representing his nation at the European and World Junior Championships.

Winning the esteemed Orange Bowl tournament in Florida in 2002 was one of Murray's junior career accomplishments. This triumph established him as one of the best junior players in the world and put him on the road to success as a professional.

Future greats like Novak Djokovic, Stan Wawrinka, and Jo-Wilfried Tsonga gave Murray serious competition. His early rivalries aided in the development of his strong work ethic and astute sense of strategy—qualities that would be crucial to his success in the workplace.

But Murray had some disappointments in his junior year of college. He battled ailments and tremendous pressure to succeed, especially from the public and British media. Still, he persisted, overcoming challenges with the help of his family and his own fortitude.

As his junior career came to an end, Murray started thinking about making the switch to professional tennis. Being a highly sought-after prospect due to his stellar junior record and developing reputation, he ultimately made the decision to turn pro in 2005. With this crucial choice, he embarked on an incredible career path that would lead him to the heights of tennis achievement.

ACHIEVEMENTS IN JUNIOR TEAMS .

Andy Murray's remarkable talent and commitment were demonstrated by his dominance in junior competitions. He topped the junior rankings by continuously outperforming his rivals and winning multiple titles and awards.

Murray's triumph at the 2003 Junior US Open, where he overcame Donald Young and Sam Querrey, future ATP stars, was one of his most spectacular wins. This victory confirmed his status as a rising star in the tennis industry and represented his first Grand Slam junior title.

Murray excelled in junior competitions outside of Grand Slam competitions. Several junior International Tennis Federation (ITF) championships were won by him, including the coveted Eddie Herr International Junior Championships in 2003. With this win, he solidified his place as the best junior player in the world and received a wildcard into the Miami Masters on the ATP tour.

Murray's outstanding athleticism, accurate shooting, and tactical awareness were the cornerstones of his junior tournament success. With his lightning-fast reflexes, deft footwork, and cunning strategies, he outwitted his opponents and frequently converted defense into attack with his superb counterpunching abilities.

As Murray's junior career developed, elite coaches, scouts, and sponsors started to take notice of him. Due to his outstanding results, he was accepted into the elite training programme of the British Lawn Tennis Association (LTA), giving him access to top-notch instruction, facilities, and equipment.

Murray's junior tournament triumphs set the stage for his eventual professional career by giving him the self-assurance, self-control, and competitive spirit he needed to be successful at the top. With his developing reputation and stellar junior record, he was well-positioned to make a smooth transition to the professional ranks, where he would have to prove himself as a top-tier tennis player in the face of fresh chances and obstacles.

ASCEND TO WORLD NO. 1 IN JUNIOR WORLD

Andy Murray's rise to the top of the junior rankings was an incredible journey that was characterized by perseverance, hard work, and a passion for perfection. Murray's rating rose rapidly as he dominated the junior circuit, and in 2004, he finally achieved the coveted top spot.

Murray's ascent to the junior world number one ranking was propelled by several noteworthy triumphs in elite competitions. He demonstrated his versatility and skill on many surfaces by winning the Junior Australian Open, Junior French Open, and Junior Wimbledon crowns.

A crucial element contributing to Murray's achievements was his flexibility in playing various styles. He created a flexible style of play that let him take advantage of his opponents' flaws and counteract their advantages. He stands out from his contemporaries due to his tactical awareness and strategic thinking, which allow him to outmaneuver even the most accomplished opponents.

Murray's ascent to the top was aided greatly by his commitment to training and fitness. He put forth a lot of effort working with his trainers and coaches to build a solid physical base that allowed him to play with a high level of energy throughout a game.

Murray became a highly sought-after player on the junior circuit as his ranking skyrocketed. He was praised as a potential star by tennis commentators and fans alike, and he was invited to participate in prestigious events like the ITF Junior Masters.

Murray's rise to the top of the junior world rankings was a noteworthy career success that showcased his extraordinary talent, strong work ethic, and devotion to the game. This feat not only cemented his status as a top prospect but also put him on the right path for future professional success.

EXCHANGE TO PROFESSIONAL TENNIS.

Andy Murray experienced a dramatic increase in the level of competition, physical demands, and mental strain when he made the switch to professional tennis. Murray said goodbye to the junior circuit and set off on a new path, conquering tough opponents, overcoming the difficulties of the ATP tour, and solidifying his place as a rising star in the tennis world.

In 2005, Murray made his professional debut against world No. 14 Tommy Robredo at the ATP tournament in Barcelona. Even though he lost in straight sets, exposure to the intensity and tempo of professional tennis proved to be crucial.

Murray experienced a challenging learning curve when navigating the ATP tour. He had to adjust and improve his game because he was up against seasoned pros, each with their own distinct style and strengths. Through intense training sessions, he improved his technique and gained a more sophisticated understanding of the game, all of which helped him perfect his skills.

Murray had a lot of ups and downs in his early professional career. He battled ailments, such as a persistent back issue, and had disappointments by losing in the first round of competitions. Nevertheless, he persisted, depending on his fortitude, work ethic, and resolute family and team support.

When Murray advanced to the ATP competition quarterfinals in San Jose, California, in 2006, it was a turning point in his career. This accomplishment was a turning moment in his career since he started to compete at a better level consistently and broke into the top 50 of the ATP rankings.

Leading coaches became interested in Murray as his professional career took off, among them Brad Gilbert, who would eventually serve as his mentor. Along the way, he started to build enduring bonds with the players who would go on to fight each other in the future, such as Rafael Nadal and Novak Djokovic.

Murray's decision to become a professional tennis player was evidence of his guts, tenacity, and love for the game. By embracing the difficulties of the ATP tour, growing from his failures, and consistently honing his skill, he laid the groundwork for a tremendous career that would lead him to the highest level of tennis achievement.

CHAPTER 3: EARLY PROFESSIONAL CAREER .

Early in his professional career, Andy Murray saw tremendous growth and development. He rose through the ranks steadily and achieved a number of key milestones that solidified his reputation as a talented young player.

Murray played his first-round match at Wimbledon in 2006, winning over Juan Carlos Ferrero to make his Grand Slam debut. This triumph was a pivotal point in his career since it showed that he could compete on the highest platform against elite opponents.

Murray's relationship with coach Brad Gilbert, who assisted him in honing his skills and adopting a more calculated approach to the game, also shaped his early professional career. Murray's ranking climbed under Gilbert's direction, breaking into the top 20 for the first time in 2007.

Murray's 2008 run to the Madrid final of the ATP Masters was one of the high points of his early career. Even though he ultimately fell short against Roger Federer, this match proved he could compete with the best players in the world and was a major turning point in his career.

But Murray had difficulties in his early professional career. In addition to dealing with injury struggles, he was under tremendous pressure from the British public and media to become the first British player to win a Grand Slam title since Fred Perry in 1936.

Murray persisted because of his commitment, his strong work ethic, and the encouragement of his teammates and family. He persisted in pushing himself, improving his technique, and increasing his level of physical fitness, laying the groundwork for an incredible career that would propel him to the pinnacle of the tennis world.

EARLY PROFESSIONAL GAME AND SUCCESS.

Andy Murray's career transition from junior tennis to the professional circuit was exemplified by his first professional matches and victories. At the 2005 ATP tournament in Barcelona, Murray made his professional debut against Tommy Robredo, the world's fourteenth-ranked player. Despite losing in straight sets, he gained crucial knowledge by seeing the ferocity and speed of professional tennis.

Shortly thereafter, in the Manchester ATP Challenger tournament, Murray won his first match as a professional. At a pivotal point in his career, he overcame Alex Bogdanovic, another British player, in straight sets. This triumph gave him more self-assurance and proved that he could compete on a professional level.

Early career matches for Murray were a learning experience as he adjusted to a more competitive level and improved his technique. He gained experience handling the demands of professional tennis by competing against seasoned opponents, including players ranked in the top 100. His initial triumphs in his professional career served as evidence of his diligence and commitment, demonstrating his aptitude and resilience to excel at the highest level.

Murray defeated Santiago Ventura, ranked 35th in the world, in one of his most significant early victories at the Newport ATP tournament. This win showed that Murray could compete against elite opponents and represented a major upset. He kept gaining ground, emerging as a rising star in the tennis world and taking home his maiden ATP Challenger trophy in Eckental, Germany.

Murray's early victories in professional contests set the stage for his later success by showcasing his ability and commitment to the game. These early triumphs gave him self-assurance and inspired him to keep striving for more, paving the way for an incredible career that would bring him to the highest level of tennis achievement.

FAILURES AND RESETTLEMENTS.

Andy Murray faced many challenges on his ascent to the top. He encountered many difficulties and disappointments despite his early accomplishments, which put his fortitude and resilience to the test.

Murray's continual struggle with injury was one of his greatest obstacles. His persistent back problem caused him to miss multiple competitions and required surgery in 2013. Murray's injury problems persisted; in 2015, he sustained a wrist injury, and in 2017, he sustained a hip injury that necessitated more surgery and a protracted recovery period.

Murray freely talked about his troubles with anxiety and sadness. Murray also had mental health issues. He was very open about the strain playing professional tennis put on his mental health. In order to concentrate on his mental health, he took a hiatus from the sport in 2019. This decision was met with a great deal of love and appreciation.

Another big blow occurred in 2014 when Murray broke out with longtime mentor Ivan Lendl. Together, they had produced two Grand Slam victories as well as an Olympic gold medal. But the two broke up, and Murray was left to look for a new coach to help him.

Murray faced difficulties in his personal life as well. He was under constant public and media scrutiny, especially in the British press, which frequently questioned his dedication to the sport and questioned his performances.

Murray persisted because of his inner fortitude, the encouragement of his loved ones, and his unshakable commitment to his profession. He kept up his diligent work, changing his approach and coming up with fresh strategies to get past his emotional and physical obstacles. Murray surmounted every challenge with tenacity and determination, growing stronger and more resilient with every year that went by.

A COMPLETION IN THE ATP TOURNAMENTS.

Andy Murray's ascent from a promising young player to a legitimate championship contender was largely influenced by his breakthrough performance in ATP events.

In the final of the 2006 SAP Open in San Jose, California, Murray defeated top-seeded Andy Roddick to win his first ATP title. This triumph was a huge turning point in his career since it proved he could compete with the best players in the world and solidified his position as a rising star in the tennis world.

In Cincinnati the following year, Murray defeated Novak Djokovic in the championship match to capture his first ATP Masters title. Murray became the first British player to win an ATP Masters championship since Fred Perry in 1937, making this triumph a historic turning point.

Murray has become increasingly successful in ATP competitions, winning titles in Shanghai, Toronto, and Madrid. In addition, he advanced to the finals of multiple Grand Slam competitions, such as Wimbledon and the Australian Open, establishing himself as one of the best players in the world.

Murray's success in ATP competitions was a result of his diligence, commitment, and tenacity. Despite countless setbacks and injuries during his career, he persisted in pushing himself to improve his skills and increase his level of physical fitness. He became the dominant power in men's tennis thanks to his success in ATP events, which was a pivotal point in his career.

The achievement also signaled a change in Murray's perspective on the game. On the court, he developed greater self-assurance and assertiveness and showed a willingness to take chances and challenge himself. Even under severe strain and in the face of hardship, his heightened resilience and self-belief allowed him to win matches

CHAPTER 4: GRAND SLAM SUCCESS.

Andy Murray's Grand Slam victory was the result of years of arduous effort, commitment, and fortitude. Although he had been on the verge of winning multiple major titles, he didn't quite make it until the 2012 US Open, when he defeated Novak Djokovic in an exciting five-set contest.

A major turning point in Murray's career came when he defeated Fred Perry in the US Open, becoming the first British player to win a Grand Slam singles championship since 1936. In the UK, there was a huge celebration following Murray's victory, and he was acclaimed as a national hero.

In 2013, Murray maintained his Grand Slam winning streak as he won Wimbledon and once again defeated Djokovic in the championship match. Given that it was Murray's first Wimbledon victory and solidified his place among the best players in British tennis history, this triumph was very meaningful.

Murray's triumphs at the US Open and Wimbledon were just two examples of his Grand Slam glory. In addition, he showed that he could compete at the highest level on all surfaces by making it to the French Open final once and the Australian Open final three times.

Murray is renowned for his remarkable athleticism, astute shot selection, and relentless commitment to the game. These traits, as well as his capacity to perform well under duress on the largest tennis stages, are demonstrated by his Grand Slam achievements.

British tennis has greatly benefited from Murray's Grand Slam triumphs, which have motivated a new generation of players and spectators alike. Because of his accomplishments, tennis has gained more attention in the UK, and his influence is still felt today.

FIRST AWARD FOR GRAND SLAM AT US OPEN.

The 2012 US Open saw Andy Murray win his maiden Grand Slam title, which was a historic milestone for British tennis. Murray eventually broke through the glass ceiling after years of hard work and determination, beating Novak Djokovic in an exciting five-set contest.

There were difficulties along the way to the title. Due to rain delays, Murray had to play four matches in five days, which was an arduous schedule. In addition, he had to get beyond a persistent knee issue that may have ended his campaign.

Murray had incredible tenacity and resolve. He used his knowledge and expertise to outmanoeuvre his rivals by producing deft shots and possessing remarkable athleticism.

It took more than four hours for the dramatic matchup against Djokovic to conclude. With remarkable mental fortitude, Murray overcame a set down to win 7-6, 7-5, 2-6, 3-6, and 6-2. Murray fell to the ground, overtaken with relief and delight, as a wave of emotion greeted the victory.

With the victory, Murray's career reached a major turning point, and his 76-year wait for a Grand Slam singles champion in Britain came to an end. It also solidified his reputation as a tennis superstar around the world, winning him a great deal of respect and recognition.

Murray's first Grand Slam victory at the US Open was evidence of his perseverance, commitment, and undying love for the game. It cemented his place in the annals of tennis history and inspired a new generation of players and spectators.

BRITISH HISTORY AND THE VICTORY AT WIMBLEDON.

Andy Murray's victory at Wimbledon in 2013 was historic and cemented his place in British tennis history. Murray became the first British player to win the men's singles title at the All England Lawn Tennis Club since Fred Perry in 1936 by defeating Novak Djokovic in the championship match.

Murray's accomplishment has enormous significance that cannot be overemphasized. He broke a 77-year British tennis drought, igniting a national celebration across the United Kingdom. Fans all throughout the country rejoiced with the win, with many praising Murray as a national hero.

Murray's victory at Wimbledon was evidence of his steadfast commitment and tenacity. He'd been this close to winning countless times before, but he'd failed. But instead of giving up, he used every setback as fuel to keep going farther and farther.

The triumph was also a testament to Murray's coach, Ivan Lendl, who had assisted him in acquiring the strategic intelligence and mental tenacity required to compete at the highest level. Murray's victory was largely due to Lendl's coaching, as he handled the tournament's obstacles with grace and assurance.

Murray's Wimbledon triumph was a watershed in British tennis history, motivating a new wave of competitors and spectators. It solidified his place among the best tennis players in British history, right up there with Virginia Wade and Fred Perry.

Murray's victory signified a noteworthy turning point in his personal path, proving that he can rise above hardship and attain greatness. His tenacity, passion, and dedication had paid off, and he now holds a legendary status in the world of tennis.

OPEN AUSTRALIA'S VICTORY.

A major turning point in Andy Murray's remarkable career was reached with his decisive victory at the 2016 Australian Open. Murray became the first British player to win the Australian Open since Fred Perry in 1937 when he defeated Novak Djokovic in the championship match.

Murray's victory served as evidence of his steadfast commitment and tenacity. Before the event, he had to overcome a lot of obstacles, such as a demanding schedule and a persistent injury. He was undeterred nonetheless and overcame every challenge with remarkable agility and mental courage.

It was an exciting match when Murray face Djokovic in the final, displaying his extraordinary skill and planning. He used a cunning strategy, outwitting his opponent with his accurate serving and astute shot placement. Murray fell to the ground, overtaken with relief and delight, as a wave of emotion greeted the victory.

Murray's victory at the Australian Open opened a new chapter in his career and showed that he could compete at the highest levels on the biggest platforms. It also solidified his place among the best tennis players in British history, right up there with Virginia Wade and Fred Perry.

The victory had a significant effect on British tennis, motivating both players and spectators of a new age. It was also a pivotal point in Murray's life story, demonstrating his fortitude and tenacity in the face of difficulty. His victory in the Australian Open will always be regarded as the pinnacle of his remarkable career.

CHAPTER 5: OLYMPIC GLORY.

Andy Murray's route to the Olympics served as evidence of his unrelenting commitment to tennis. He had always hoped to represent Great Britain in sports on the biggest platform, and his dedication and hard work paid off handsomely.

Murray participated in the singles and doubles competitions at the 2008 Beijing Olympics for his maiden Olympic participation. Even though he didn't win a medal, the experience was priceless, and he went back to the Olympics in 2012 with an intense will to win.

Murray met Roger Federer in the London 2012 Olympics final, seeking retribution for his Wimbledon defeat earlier in the summer. In straight sets, he took home the gold medal, solidifying his legacy as a British Olympian.

After overcoming Juan Martin del Potro in an exciting final four years later at the Rio 2016 Olympics, Murray made history as the first tennis player to win back-to-back Olympic singles titles. The fact that

Murray prevailed cemented his reputation as a national hero and created a historic moment for British tennis.

Murray's accomplishments at the Olympics extended beyond his success in singles. Alongside Laura Robson, he also took home a silver medal at the London 2012 Olympics in the mixed doubles competition.

Murray's Olympic journey showcased his extraordinary talent, mental fortitude, and commitment to his trade. His Olympic success left a lasting legacy in the tennis world, inspiring a new generation of players and spectators.

2012 LONDON GOLD MEDALS .

Andy Murray's gold medal win at the 2012 London Olympics was an incredible occasion that solidified his place in British sports history. Murray took on Roger Federer, the man he had fallen short of in the Wimbledon final a few weeks prior, on a bright afternoon at Wimbledon's Centre Court.

Murray, though, was determined to write a different script this time. He played arguably the finest tennis of his life, outwitting Federer in straight sets (6-2, 6-1, 6-4), with the fans firmly behind him. With the triumph, Murray became the first British tennis player to win an Olympic gold medal in singles since Josiah Ritchie in 1908, making it a historic milestone for British tennis.

The emotions were evident as Murray stood on the stage, taking in the national anthem and being awarded his gold medal. His triumphant Olympic gold was the realization of his desire, and his expression was marked with pride and accomplishment. The win was not just a testimonial to his own success but also to the steadfast support of his coaches, family, and the whole British people.

Murray's career underwent a dramatic shift after winning the gold medal in London in 2012. He went on to rule the tennis world and motivate a new breed of players and supporters. His Olympic success will always be seen as the pinnacle of his remarkable career and as the occasion that cemented his legacy in British sports history.

DEFENSE OF THE RIO 2016 GOLD MEDALS.

Andy Murray's Olympic gold medal defense in Rio de Janeiro in 2016 was an incredible demonstration of tenacity and fortitude. Murray had a difficult challenge in Brazil following his historic triumph in London in 2012: he had to become the first tennis player to win back-to-back Olympic gold medals in singles.

Murray faced some difficulties on his trip to Rio. He overcame a persistent injury that threatened to end his campaign and dealt with a demanding schedule that involved playing several games in a short amount of time. He used his experience and mental toughness to overcome the challenges, nevertheless, and refused to give up.

In the final, Murray played Juan Martin del Potro, a strong opponent who had pushed him to the edge in their previous matches. Both players gave it their best in a fierce, high-stakes struggle, making the match an exciting affair. Murray prevailed in a close three-set match (7-5, 4-6, 6-2) thanks to his superior fitness and tactical play.

Murray's victorious gold medal defense served as evidence of his steadfast commitment to and love of the game of tennis. He had triumphed over hardship and established himself as one of the best tennis players of all time. A flood of emotions greeted the victory as Murray revealed in the glory of his historic accomplishment with his team and family.

Murray's defense of the gold medal in Rio 2016 was a major turning point in his career that cemented his reputation as a tennis great and motivated a new breed of players and spectators. His outstanding accomplishments will always be regarded as the pinnacle of his storied career.

OLYMPIC LEGACY AND SIGNIFICANCE.

Both Andy Murray's professional and personal lives have been significantly impacted by his Olympic experience. Murray feels a great deal of pride and inspiration from representing Great Britain on the biggest sporting stage.

With the Olympics, Murray has a rare chance to reach out to a wider audience outside of the tennis world. Using his position to advocate for the values of perseverance, commitment, and collaboration, he has embraced the Olympic ideals of excellence, camaraderie, and respect.

British tennis has greatly benefited from Murray's Olympic victory, which has inspired a new generation of players and spectators alike. Tennis involvement has increased as a result of Murray's successes; many aspiring players look up to him as an inspiration and role model.

Murray has personally benefited from the Olympic experience, which has taught him important lessons about tenacity, fortitude, and the value of friends and family. He has acknowledged that the Olympics have contributed to his growth in terms of perspective and sense of purpose, both on and off the court.

Murray's participation in the Olympics has promoted a feeling of camaraderie and kinship among sportsmen from many sports. With his Olympic teammates, he has forged enduring relationships based on mutual support and experience sharing throughout both the highs and lows of competition.

For Andy Murray, both his professional and personal lives have been profoundly shaped by his Olympic experience. It has greatly influenced British tennis as well as the larger sporting community, and it has motivated him to achieve new heights both on and off the court.

CHAPTER 6: COACHING AND TEAM.

In addition to his own skill and diligence, Andy Murray's success on the court is also ascribed to the hardworking group of teammates that support him. Throughout his career, his coaching staff has been a crucial part of his development, offering advice, encouragement, and knowledge.

The most illustrious coaching duo for Murray was with tennis great Ivan Lendl. Murray's aggressive playing style improved under Lendl's guidance and experience, and this helped him win some of his most memorable matches, including the Wimbledon title in 2013 and the gold medal at the 2012 Olympics.

Murray has also worked with Brad Gilbert, Miles MacLagan, and Jamie Delgado as coaches, in addition to Lendl. Murray has been able to adjust to the constantly shifting professional tennis scene thanks to the distinct perspectives and tactics that each coach has offered.

Murray has more teammates than only his coaches. His mother, Judy Murray, in particular, has been a consistent source of encouragement and support. Kim Sears, his wife, has also been an essential collaborator, offering him stability and emotional support throughout his professional life.

In order to make sure Murray is both physically and psychologically ready for competition, his squad also consists of a network of trainers, physiotherapists, and mental performance coaches. Murray has been able to perform at the highest level despite difficulties because of his team's combined effort.

It is impossible to overestimate the role that teamwork played in Murray's success. Throughout his journey, his coaches, family, and support system have all been essential in assisting him in overcoming obstacles and realizing his objectives. Murray's squad continues to be an essential part of his success as he develops both as a player and as a person.

COLLABORATION WITH IVAN LENDL

Ivan Lendl and Andy Murray's collaboration changed the course of Murray's career. The legendary tennis player and former world number one, Ivan Lendl, contributed a plethora of knowledge and experience to their coaching partnership.

When the two started working together in 2012, their collaboration was crucial to Murray's growth. Murray's mental toughness, strategic play, and general confidence on the court all improved under Lendl's tutelage.

A crucial element of their collaboration was Lendl's capacity to empathize with Murray's circumstances. As a former player, Lendl was able to provide Murray with specific guidance and assistance because he was aware of the demands and difficulties Murray experienced.

It was Lendl who helped Murray's game take off. He ended Britain's 77-year wait for a male singles winner by winning many trophies, including the Wimbledon crown in 2013 and the gold medal at the 2012 Olympics.

Lendl's influence went beyond tactics and approach. He encouraged Murray to embrace his skills and have faith in his abilities, which helped him adopt a more optimistic outlook.

Their collaboration was based on mutual respect, trust, and candid communication. Murray's fiery attitude was counterbalanced by Lendl's cool-headedness and collected manner, resulting in a harmonious and fruitful coaching partnership.

As one of the most fruitful coaching partnerships in tennis history, the Lendl-Murray alliance stands as a monument to the importance of mentorship and teamwork in reaching greatness.

OTHER MENTORS AND COACHES.

Although Ivan Lendl played a significant role in Andy Murray's coaching career, he wasn't the only notable mentor in his path. Murray has worked with several other coaches and mentors who have contributed significantly to his growth and success.

Among them is the well-known tennis coach Brad Gilbert, who coached Murray from 2006 to 2007. Gilbert gave Murray more of an aggressive playing style and assisted him in honing his offensive abilities.

Murray collaborated with British coach Miles MacLagan, who guided him from 2007 to 2010. Murray's early success was greatly aided by MacLagan, who saw him through to his first Grand Slam final at the 2008 US Open.

Murray has also consulted mental performance experts for advice. Robbie Anderson, a sports psychologist who has been working with Murray since 2012, is one such mentor. Murray can now function at his peak under duress thanks to Anderson's assistance in helping him cultivate mental toughness and strategic thinking.

Murray has acknowledged that his mother, Judy Murray, in particular, had a big impact on his career. Judy, a former tennis player herself, introduced Andy and his brother Jamie to the sport and has been a steady source of support and encouragement throughout their careers.

Murray has become one of the most successful tennis players of his generation as a result of the varied viewpoints and professional backgrounds of these teachers and mentors.

AID THE FAMILY AND THE TEAM.

Andy Murray's family and network of supporters have been crucial to his success, giving his career a solid start. Specifically, his family has consistently provided support and direction.

Judy Murray, Murray's mother, has had a significant influence on both his life and profession. Judy, who used to play tennis herself, introduced Andy and his brother Jamie to the game and has been a huge advocate for them ever since. Throughout his career, Andy has found great motivation in her unshakable conviction in his ability.

Murray's father, William Murray, has been extremely important in his life by giving him a sense of security and regularity away from the demands of professional tennis.

Throughout their marriage, Andy has found emotional stability and support from his wife, Kim Sears. Her influence has been credited with helping Andy adopt a more optimistic outlook and has helped him manage the highs and lows of his profession.

Behind the scenes, a committed team of specialists works diligently to support Murray. Patricio Apey, his agent, has been crucial in helping him manage his career and win lucrative endorsements and contract negotiations.

Mark Bender, Murray's physiotherapist, has been instrumental in helping him stay strong and fit throughout his career. Murray has been able to recover from injuries and maintain his physical conditioning because of Bender's knowledge, which has improved his performance on the court.

Murray's success has been largely attributed to the support he has received from his family, team, and mentors. This has given him a solid professional foundation and enabled him to accomplish his objectives.

CHAPTER 7: INJURIES AND CHALLENGES.

Throughout his career, Andy Murray has faced numerous obstacles and injuries that have put his fortitude and resilience to the test. Murray has experienced multiple obstacles that have threatened to impede his career, despite his talent and effort.

Murray struggled for years with a back problem, which was one of his biggest setbacks. The injury first appeared in 2012, and in 2013, surgery was necessary. Murray battled to regain his form and fitness during his protracted and difficult recuperation.

Murray was forced to retire from the French Open in 2016 due to a shoulder issue. Murray had a serious injury, which was unfortunate because he had been playing well before the competition.

Murray has also struggled with his mental health. He disclosed in 2018 that he has been seeing a therapist for assistance with his anxiety and sadness.

In addition to harming his tennis career, Murray's struggles and injuries have also had an impact on his personal life. He has openly discussed how his injuries have affected his relationships and general well-being.

Murray has demonstrated incredible tenacity and resolve. He has put in a great deal of effort to heal his wounds and get well mentally. His bravery and tenacity have won him a great deal of respect and adoration from a vast number of followers.

Murray's outlook on his life and profession has changed. He now understands the value of mental health and the necessity of putting his own well-being first. Through his experiences, he has also become a more understanding and encouraging friend and coworker. He has also used his platform to spread the word about mental health issues and lessen the stigma associated with them.

RECOVERY AND BACK SURGERY.

Andy Murray underwent back surgery in September 2013, marking a crucial turning point in his injury journey. Murray did not make the decision to have surgery lightly, but his sciatica and chronic back pain had become incapacitating, impairing his quality of life and performance.

Dr. Robert Bray of Los Angeles conducted the procedure with the intention of repairing a bulging disc in Murray's lower back and relieving pressure on his sciatic nerve. Although the treatment was successful, recovery took a lengthy time.

Murray's recovery from surgery took a long time and called for perseverance, self-control, and commitment. He had to undergo intense physical therapy to strengthen his core and increase his flexibility after spending several weeks in a brace that prevented him from bending or twisting.

Murray's early rehabilitation was difficult since he had a hard time accepting his new physical limits. But he started to improve little by little, gaining his strength and mobility back.

Murray's recuperation was greatly aided by his support system, including his physiotherapist, Mark Bender, who put in a lot of effort to create a personalised rehabilitation plan. Murray received invaluable advice and support from his coach, Ivan Lendl, who also helped him remain motivated and focused during the process.

Murray's back was stronger and more resilient than ever when he eventually made a comeback to the tennis court after several months of rehabilitation. He had learned a lot from the experience, including the value of putting his physical and emotional health first and how to persevere.

Murray became a stronger, more motivated, and more grateful person as a result of his back surgery and recuperation, which had a significant effect on both his personal and professional life.

OTHER INJURIES AND SETBACKS.

Throughout his career, Andy Murray has experienced numerous injuries and setbacks in addition to his back surgery. These difficulties have put his mental fortitude and resolve to the test, in addition to his physical toughness.

One such setback occurred when he had to withdraw from the 2015 Davis Cup quarterfinals due to a wrist injury. Prior to the event, Murray was in superb shape; therefore, his chances of leading Great Britain to victory were severely damaged by the injury.

Murray had to pull out of the Miami Open in 2016 due to a calf issue. He struggled to recapture his form in the weeks that followed, which was a setback in his preparation for the clay court season.

Murray has also sustained a number of ankle sprains, including a serious one that required him to retire from the 2018 Australian Open. Murray had been playing well before the competition, so the injury was a major setback.

Murray has experienced a number of other setbacks, such as shingles in 2017 and a minor knee injury in 2019. His mental and physical health have been impacted by these difficulties, which have also put his will to achieve at the top to the test.

Murray has continuously shown his tenacity and resolve, putting in great effort to heal his wounds and restore his form. His career has been distinguished by his capacity to overcome adversity, which has won him the respect and affection of many people and inspired innumerable supporters.

MENTAL FITNESS AND SUCCESS.

In addition to physical wounds, Andy Murray's journey has been characterized by a strong dedication to mental health and wellness. Murray's mental health has occasionally suffered as a result of the intense strain and scrutiny he has endured as a professional athlete.

In 2018, Murray disclosed that he has been seeing a therapist in order to address his issues with anxiety and despair. This brave revelation encouraged many people to get help and helped spread awareness about mental health in sports.

Since then, Murray has turned into a mental health campaigner, utilising his position to dispel stigma and encourage wellbeing. He has collaborated with nonprofits and charities that support mental health, sharing his personal stories and providing assistance to people in need.

Murray's attitude towards tennis has also been impacted by his dedication to mental health. He has made self-care a priority and included mindfulness, yoga, and meditation in his training regimen. He has been able to control his stress and keep a good work-life balance thanks to this all-encompassing strategy.

A new generation of players and people has been motivated to prioritize their mental health by Murray's candid discussion of his challenges and emphasis on mental wellness. His bravery and openness have contributed to a change in sports culture that emphasizes the value of mental health in addition to physical fitness.

Murray has demonstrated that getting treatment is a sign of strength rather than weakness and that mental health is equally as essential as physical health. His activism has benefited many people outside of his professional career by contributing to the development of a more encouraging and welcoming atmosphere in sports.

CHAPTER 8: OFF-COURT VENTURES.

Due in large part to his achievements on the tennis court, Andy Murray has been able to demonstrate his entrepreneurial spirit and love of innovation through a variety of off-court endeavors.

Murray established his management firm, 77 Management, in 2013, and it currently represents a select roster of sportsmen and celebrities. Through this business, he is able to use his contacts and experience to help other people advance their careers.

Murray has also made investments in a number of companies, including a share in Hibernian FC, a professional football team in Scotland. His conviction in the club's future and his dedication to promoting Scottish sport are evident in this investment.

Murray has teamed up with well-known companies like Standard Life, Head, and Under Armour to represent them globally. Through these collaborations, he has been able to promote goods and services that share his values while also strengthening his own brand.

Murray invested in PlayerData, a Scottish digital business that specializes in wearable technology and data analytics for sports, because of his enthusiasm for innovation. His interest in the nexus between sport and technology is evident in this investment.

IMurray has worked with the Andy Murray Foundation, a nonprofit organization his family started to help underprivileged kids in Scotland. His passion for aiding the next generation and giving back to his community is evident in his work with the foundation.

Murray's endeavors outside of the court bear witness to his aptitude for entrepreneurship, love of creativity, and commitment to helping people. His brand has grown as a result of these endeavors, which have also given him the opportunity to positively influence others off the tennis court.

CHARITY WORK AND PHILANTHROPY.

Since 2014, Murray has served as a UNICEF UK Ambassador. In March 2022, Murray raised over £500,000 by donating his prize money from the 2022 competition to aid the children of Ukraine. He is in favor of United For Wildlife, a nonprofit organization that seeks to mobilize people all around the world to change the way that wildlife is protected.

Along with David Beckham, Murray serves on the leadership council of Malaria No More UK and has contributed millions of dollars to the cause.

Murray took part in the 'Rally for Bally' event, which raised funds for the Elena Baltacha Academy of Tennis and the Royal Marsden Cancer Charity. He was appointed a WWF ambassador in November 2014, and since then, he has backed a number of WWF programmes, such as Earth Hour in 2015.

Murray demonstrated his support for Earth Hour in 2015, a global chance to show care for the planet and its biodiversity.

Murray joined the Digital Health and Care Institute, a Scotland-based organization, in July 2016 as an advocate for global digital health and wellness. His philanthropic initiatives illustrate his passion for giving back and making a positive impact on the world.

PERSONAL LIFE AND INTERESTS.

Andy Murray's personal life and interests outside of tennis are varied and representative of his personality. Murray is a loving father to their four children and a committed husband to Kim Sears. Murray frequently spends his free time with his family, cherishing special moments spent away from the tennis court. The family resides in Surrey, England.

Murray is a passionate music enthusiast who appreciates listening to a variety of styles, such as pop, rock, and classical music. He has also gone to gigs by the Scottish rock group Travis, whom he especially likes.

Murray is an ardent football enthusiast who cheers for the Scottish team, Hibernian FC. He is so dedicated to Scottish sport that he has even made investments in the club.

Murray is a voracious reader who likes to read both non-fiction and historical fiction. He has stated that Guy Gavriel Kay's "The Lions of Al-Rassan" is his favourite novel.

Murray has a deep appreciation for art and has amassed a collection of different works throughout the years. In his spare time, he has visited nearby art galleries and demonstrated his support for emerging artists.

Murray's hobbies and personal life demonstrate his multifaceted nature and the different facets that contribute to his overall well-roundedness outside of the tennis world.

CHAPTER 9: LAW AND IMPACT.

There is no denying Andy Murray's influence and legacy in tennis and beyond. He has inspired innumerable young players and spectators worldwide as a tennis champion. His commitment, tenacity, and love for the game have elevated him to the status of an inspiration to many.

Murray has had a significant influence on British tennis. He's been a trailblazer, setting an example for future British athletes to chase after. Tennis participation in the UK has increased as a result of his success, and his legacy is still motivating a new generation of players.

Murray's impact goes beyond the game of tennis. He has been a strong supporter of social justice and gender equality, using his position to spread the word about these vital issues. His dedication to philanthropy and altruistic endeavors has profoundly impacted several lives.

Murray's services to the tennis community are another aspect of his legacy. He has pushed to strengthen the organization and administration of the sport and fought for the welfare of the players. For many years to come, his influence on the game will be felt.

Murray has gotten many honors for his accomplishments, including a knighthood in 2017. In addition, he has won the Freedom of the City of Stirling and been nominated for BBC Sports Personality of the Year on several occasions.

Andy Murray's impact and legacy bear witness to his enthusiasm, hard work, and dedication. He will always be regarded as one of the best tennis players of all time, and future generations will be inspired by and shaped by his influence on the game.

IMPACT ON TENNIS IN BRITAIN.

Andy Murray has had a significant and enduring influence on British tennis. He has motivated a new generation of players and spectators by being the first male British player to win a Grand Slam singles title in more than 75 years.

The number of tennis players in the UK has significantly increased as a result of Murray's success. Since Murray's 2013 Wimbledon victory, junior tennis participation has increased by more than 20%, according to the Lawn Tennis Association (LTA). The number of tennis clubs, coaches, and facilities has increased nationwide as a result of this increase in interest.

Murray has had an impact at the local level as well. His charity, the Andy Murray Foundation, has contributed to a number of programmes designed to give underprivileged kids and teenagers more access to tennis. As a result, tennis is now a more varied and inclusive sport in the UK.

Because of Murray's accomplishments, British tennis is now more well-known worldwide. He has represented British tennis with distinction, highlighting the skill and long history of the sport in the nation. Because of his performance, there is now more money invested in British tennis. The LTA announced a large increase in financing for elite player development and grassroots programmes.

The Davis Cup has also been impacted by Murray; in 2015, Great Britain won the championship for the first time in more than 70 years. This triumph demonstrated Murray's leadership and the development of British tennis.

In 2016, Murray received the President's Award from the LTA for his services to British tennis. A new generation of players and spectators is encouraged to take up the sport by his legacy, which is still shaping the sport in the UK.

INSPIRATION AND ROLE MODEL.

The influence of Andy Murray goes much beyond his stellar tennis career. Beyond the realm of sports, he has inspired and served as a role model for millions of others. People from many walks of life find inspiration and hope in him because of his commitment, tenacity, and enthusiasm.

Murray's ascent to the top is a result of his perseverance and hard work. He has demonstrated that everything is achievable with hard work and devotion. Numerous young athletes and spectators have been motivated to pursue their aspirations by his accomplishments, regardless of how difficult they may seem.

Murray's bravery in being candid about his battles with mental illness and injuries has lowered stigma and inspired others to get treatment when they need it. Because of his sensitivity, he has become a more lovable and sympathetic character, encouraging others to be more forthright and honest about their own hardships.

Murray's dedication to philanthropic endeavours and philanthropy has also had a big influence. His advocacy for a range of causes, including mental health organisations and charities for children, has motivated others to become involved and change the world.

As an inspiration, Murray has demonstrated that being successful involves more than just reaching greatness; it also involves leveraging one's position to change the world for the better. A new generation of youth has been motivated by him to follow their passions, put in a lot of effort, and use their skills to change the world.

Murray has won multiple honours, including the Helen Rollason Award for Sports Personality of the Year in recognition of his exceptional contributions to sports. His influence and motivation continue to uplift people all throughout the world, solidifying his status as a genuine inspiration and role model, both on and off the court.

CONTRIBUTIONS FROM THE TENNIS INDUSTRY.

Andy Murray has made substantial and wide-ranging contributions to the tennis world. He has had a significant influence on the sport as a champion, businessman, and philanthropist.

Tennis has become more and more popular in the UK and elsewhere, thanks in large part to Murray. A new generation of players and spectators has been motivated by his success, which has raised participation and viewership. Additionally, he has been instrumental in the expansion of tennis in Scotland by backing grassroots development efforts.

Tennis technology has seen significant advancements, thanks to Murray. He has partnered with and invested in a number of tennis-related enterprises, such as a maker of tennis balls and a tennis analytics platform. These initiatives have improved player performance and fan engagement by fostering innovation in the sport.

Murray has also significantly improved the administration of tennis. He has worked closely with the ATP and ITF to enhance the governance and structure of the sport and has been an advocate for player rights. His impact has shaped tennis's course and ensured that it will continue to be a popular and sustainable sport for upcoming generations.

Murray has fought hard to promote gender parity in the game of tennis. He has been a strong advocate for equal pay and opportunities for female players in tennis as well as for women's tennis. His backing has increased awareness of women's tennis and served as an inspiration to a new wave of female players and supporters.

Murray has won various honors, such as the Arthur Ashe Humanitarian Award from the ATP. His influence is still shaping tennis today, encouraging equality, creativity, and expansion across the globe.

CHAPTER 10: LATER CAREER AND RETIREMENT.

Andy Murray faced and overcame more difficulties as he moved into the later phases of his career. He struggled with injuries and had patchy play, but he was still a formidable opponent in the tennis world.

Murray made the announcement in 2019 that he would give up professional tennis after the Wimbledon Championships, citing persistent hip issues and a need to put his family and health first. The tennis community was shocked to hear the news, and players, coaches, and fans all extended their condolences.

Murray's last match was a memorable occasion in tennis history. Despite his valiant efforts, he was ultimately defeated by Roberto Bautista Agut in the Wimbledon first round. The crowded stadium gave Murray a standing ovation as he exited the court for the last time, demonstrating his lasting influence on the game.

Murray has continued to be active in tennis after retirement, taking on different endeavors and initiatives. He has shared his knowledge and perspectives with a larger audience as a tennis pundit and analyst. In an effort to nurture fresh talent and provide the upcoming generation of players with opportunities, Murray has also opened his own tennis academy.

Murray has persisted in being a strong voice for gender equality and social justice, using his position to promote and increase awareness of pertinent issues. His unwavering commitment to philanthropy and philanthropic work has inspired many people and organizations to follow in his footsteps.

Murray can be proud of his numerous accomplishments and the lasting impression he has made on the tennis world as he considers his incredible career. His reputation as one of the greatest tennis players of all time will be cemented as his legacy inspires and motivates upcoming generations of players, coaches, and fans.

SUBSEQUENT TOURS ON THE ATP TOUR.

Andy Murray faced tough competition on the ATP Tour as he progressed into the later phases of his career. He was a fearsome opponent on the court, renowned for his wit and cunning, despite his advanced age and lingering injuries.

Murray had a serious setback in 2018 when he had hip surgery, which prevented him from playing for several months. Nevertheless, he persisted in trying to heal his ailment and rejoin the tour, working nonstop.

Murray faced a new breed of players after his comeback, including Daniil Medvedev, Alexander Zverev, and Stefanos Tsitsipas. Even if he had trouble regaining his previous level of dominance, he was still able to display flashes of genius, such as his exciting win over Juan Martin del Potro at the 2019 Wimbledon Championships.

A string of farewell events characterized Murray's later years on the ATP Tour as he said goodbye to the locations and towns that had been so important to his career. He received emotional tributes and standing ovations at every location, which is evidence of his ongoing appeal and respect among tennis players.

Due to his good sportsmanship, sense of humor, and kind heart, Murray was still a highly regarded character on the circuit. His reputation as one of the greatest tennis players of all time was already solidified, and as his career came to a conclusion, he was praised by both opponents and fans.

FUTURE PLANS AND RETIREMENT.

With his announcement of his retirement from professional tennis, Andy Murray put an end to an era and started a new one. He said goodbye to the sport that had shaped him for so long and eagerly anticipated what lay ahead.

Murray has expressed in the open that he wants to continue playing tennis, just in a different way. In an effort to mold the upcoming generation of tennis stars, he has indicated an interest in teaching and mentoring young athletes.

Murray has made references to a possible career in broadcasting, where he would use his eloquent manner and wealth of knowledge to establish himself as a top tennis analyst and pundit. His perceptive analysis and affable demeanor have already established him as a popular figure among both spectators and admirers.

Murray has also mentioned his love of business and entrepreneurship, making references to possible forays into the fields of sustainability and technology. His investments in numerous startups and businesses, together with his interests in them, have already proven that he has a sharp eye for innovation and expansion.

Murray will continue to play a significant role in philanthropy and charity endeavors after retirement. He has long been an advocate for a number of causes, such as mental health organizations and charities that help children. He is clearly going to remain committed to giving back and changing the world in the years to come.

Murray has the love and support of his family, friends, and fans as he starts this new chapter in his life. Although he will always be remembered as one of the greatest tennis players of all time, there is little doubt that his influence and impact will go much beyond the tennis court.

THOUGHTS ON A SUCCESSFUL PROFESSION.

Andy Murray feels a sense of satisfaction, thankfulness, and accomplishment as he reflects on his remarkable career. Murray's career has been filled with several victories and significant events, spanning from his early years as a teenage prodigy to his reign as a tennis champion.

Murray's steadfast commitment, never-ending passion, and unflinching perseverance have characterized his career. Despite all of the difficulties and disappointments he has experienced—including injuries and losses—he has always come out stronger and more motivated.

Murray's capacity for change and adaptation has proven to be one of his strongest suits. In order to keep ahead of the competition, he has constantly improved his technique and broadened his range of shots and tactics. He has been able to outwit and outmaneuver even the most dangerous opponents thanks to his brilliance, ingenuity, and problem-solving abilities.

Murray's influence on tennis goes much beyond his long list of victories and honors. His special combination of skill, work ethic, and sportsmanship has inspired a generation of athletes, spectators, and coaches. His dedication to the sport has increased its visibility and drawn in new sponsors and spectators.

Murray is conscious of the help and direction he has received during his career as he looks back on it. He is appreciative of his family, coaches, and team for their consistent support, which has been crucial to his success. In addition, he recognises the insightful lessons he has gained from his peers and competitors, who have inspired him to improve and pursue greatness.

Murray's legacy will be shaped by both the man he has become and his accomplishments on the court. He is a well-liked figure in the tennis community because of his honesty, modesty, and friendliness, and his influence will last long after he retires.

CONCLUSIONS.

 The life story of Andy Murray is proof of the strength of perseverance, passion, and determination. Murray's career has been filled with several victories and significant events, spanning from his early years as a teenage tennis prodigy to his reign as a tennis champion.

Murray has shown an unshakable dedication to perfection by always challenging himself to get better and adjust in a sport that is changing quickly. As one of the best tennis players of all time, he has outmaneuvered even the toughest opponents thanks to his brilliance, inventiveness, and problem-solving abilities.

Murray's influence on tennis goes much beyond his long list of victories and honors. His special combination of skill, work ethic, and sportsmanship has inspired a generation of athletes, spectators, and coaches. His dedication to the sport has increased its visibility and drawn in new sponsors and spectators.

However, Murray's influence goes beyond the tennis field. He has been a strong supporter of social justice and gender equality, using his position to spread the word about these vital issues. Many people's lives have been profoundly impacted by his commitment to philanthropy and humanitarian work, and others have been motivated to follow in his footsteps.

Murray feels a sense of success, thankfulness, and pride as he looks to the future. His life story serves as a helpful reminder that accomplishments alone do not define success; rather, it is the person we become along the way.

Murray is a well-liked figure in the tennis community because of his honesty, modesty, and kindness, and his influence will last long after he retires.

The life story of Andy Murray is an inspiration to the human spirit, showing us that we can all succeed if we have a strong work ethic, perseverance, and a love for what we do. His reputation as one of the greatest tennis players of all time will be cemented as his legacy inspires and motivates upcoming generations.

The life story of Andy Murray is one of achievement, tenacity, and commitment. It serves as a reminder that perseverance is what matters and that neither victory nor failure are ultimate.

Many people all throughout the world have been inspired by Murray's journey, and future generations will continue to be impacted by his legacy. His life story is a tribute to the strength of the human spirit, and his dedication to social justice, philanthropy, and tennis has had a profound effect on the world.

Printed in Great Britain
by Amazon